# THE BOWL OF SAKI

# THE BOWL OF SAKI

**Sufi Inayat Khan**

First edition 1921
© 1921 International Headquarters of the Sufi Movement
Geneva, Switzerland

Second edition 1936
© 1936 International Headquarters of the Sufi Movement
Geneva, Switzerland

Third edition 1958
© 1958 International Headquarters of the Sufi Movement
Geneva, Switzerland

This fourth and revised edition published by
the Sufi Publishing Company, Ltd.
© 1979 International Headquarters of the Sufi Movement
Geneva, Switzerland

Library of Congress Catalog Number 78-65653
ISBN 978-0-900217-12-8 (pbk.)
ISBN 978-1-68442-283-8 (hc)

**January 1.**

As water in a fountain rises as one stream
but falls in many drops divided by time and space,-
so are the revelations of the one stream of truth.

**January 2.**

All names and forms are the garbs and covers
under which the one life is hidden.

**January 3.**

Truth without a veil
is always uninteresting to the human mind.

**January 4.**

When you stand with your back to the sun
your shadow is before you,
but when you turn and face the sun
your shadow falls behind.


**January 5.**

No one has seen God and lived.
To see God we must be non-existent.


**January 6.**

The truth cannot be spoken.
That which can be spoken is not the truth.

**January 7.**

The only power for the mystic
is the power of love.

**January 8.**

If people but knew their own religion
how tolerant they would become
and how free from any grudge
against the religion of others.

**January 9.**

The real meaning of crucifixion is to crucify
the false self that the true self may rise.
As long as the false self is not crucified
the true self is not realised.

**January 10.**

An ideal is beyond explanation;
to analyse God is to dethrone God.

**January 11.**

Where the flame of love rises
the knowledge of God unfolds of itself.

**January 12.**

Peace is perfected activity. That is perfect
which is complete in all its aspects,
balanced in each direction
and under complete control of the will.

## January 13.

Do not limit God to your virtue;
he is beyond your virtues, o pious ones.

## January 14.

A man's inclination
is the root of the tree of his life.

## January 15.

Yes, teach your principles of good,
but do not think to limit God within them.
The goodness of each man is peculiar to himself.

**January 16.**

To learn to adopt the standard of God, and to cease to wish to make the world conform to one's own standard of good is the chief lesson of religion.

**January 17.**

Thought draws the line of fate.

**January 18.**

Subtlety produces beauty; it is subtlety which is the curl of the Beloved.

**January 19.**

A king is ever a king,
be he crowned with a jewelled crown
or clad in beggar's garb.

**January 20.**

To treat every human being as a shrine of God
is to fulfil all religion.

**January 21.**

The wise man should keep the balance
between love and power,
keep the love in his nature
ever increasing and expanding
and at the same time strengthen the will
so that the heart may not easily be broken.

**January 22.**

Failure comes when will surrenders to reason.

**January 23.**

Success comes when reason (the store
of experience) surrenders to will.

**January 24.**

There is an answer to every call.
To those who call on God, God comes.

**January 25.**

He who thinks against his own desire
is his own enemy.

**January 26.**

The brain speaks through words,
the heart in the glance of the eyes
and the soul through a radiance
that charges the atmosphere, magnetizing all.

**January 27.**

Love is the merchandise
which all the world demands.
If you store it in your heart
every soul will become your customer.

**January 28.**

Sincerity is the jewel
that forms in the shell of the heart.

**January 29.**

Self-pity is the worst poverty.
It overwhelms man until he sees nothing
but illness, trouble and pain.

**January 30.**

The heart is not living
until it has experienced pain.

16

## January 31.

The pleasures of life are blinding.
It is love alone
that clears the rust from the heart,
the mirror of the soul.

## February 1.

The pain of love
is the dynamite that breaks up the heart,
even if it were as hard as a rock.

## February 2.

Our virtues are made by love
and our sins are caused by the lack of it.

**February 3.**

Love is the essence
of all religion, mysticism and philosophy.

**February 4.**

The mind is a world, a world that man makes;
and in it he will live in the hereafter
as a spider lives in the web it has woven.

**February 5.**

Mysticism without devotion is like
uncooked food: it can never be assimilated.

**February 6.**

He who stores evil in his heart cannot see beauty.

**February 7.**

The wise man, by studying nature,
enters into unity through its variety
and realises the personality of God
by sacrificing his own.

**February 8.**

Love manifests towards those whom we like
as love,
towards those whom we do not like as forgiveness.

### February 9.

Love brought man from the world of unity
to that of variety, and the same force
can take him back again to the world of unity
from the world of variety.

### February 10.

Whoever knows the mystery of vibrations
indeed knows all things.

### February 11.

He who arrives at the state of indifference without
experiencing interest in life is incomplete and apt
to be tempted by interest at any moment. But he
who arrives at the state of indifference by going
through interest really attains the blessed state.

**February 12.**

Wisdom is greater
and more difficult to attain
than intellect, piety or spirituality.


**February 13.**

Wisdom is intelligence in its pure essence,
which is not necessarily dependent upon
the knowledge of names and forms.


**February 14.**

Man forms his future by his actions.
His every good or bad action spreads its vibrations
and becomes known throughout the universe.

**February 15.**

The universe is like a dome,-
it vibrates to that which you say in it
and answers the same back to you.
So also is the law of action:
we reap what we sow.

**February 16.**

We are always searching for God far away
when all the while he is nearer to us
than our soul.

**February 17.**

Concentration and contemplation are great things.
But no contemplation is greater
than the life we have about us every day.

**February 18.**

He who expects to change the world
will be disappointed; he must change his view.
When this is done, then tolerance will come,
forgiveness will come
and there will be nothing he cannot bear.

**February 19.**

To renounce what we cannot gain
is not true renunciation,- it is weakness.

**February 20.**

The religion of each
is the attainment of his soul's desire.
When he is on the path of that attainment
he is religious. When he is off that path
he is impious.

**February 21.**

The reformer comes to plough the ground,
the prophet comes to sow the seed
and the priest comes to reap the harvest.

**February 22.**

Life is an opportunity given to satisfy
the hunger and thirst of the soul.

**February 23.**

Truth alone can succeed.
Falsehood is a waste of time and loss of energy.

**February 24.**

Do not fear God
but consciously regard
his pleasure and displeasure.

**February 25.**

He who has failed himself has failed all.
He who has conquered himself has won all.

**February 26.**

As man rises above passion,
so he begins to know love.

**February 27.**

Believe in God with childlike faith,
for simplicity with intelligence
is the sign of the holy ones.

**February 28.**

He who can live up to his ideal
is the king of life.
He who cannot is life's slave.

**February 29.**

Every moment of our life is
an invaluable opportunity.

**March 1.**

Nature speaks louder
than the call from the minaret.

**March 2.**

The priest gives a benediction from the church.
The branches of a tree
in bending give blessing from God.

**March 3.**

The soul brings its light from heaven,
the mind acquires its knowledge from earth.
Therefore, when the soul believes readily,
the mind may still doubt.

## March 4.

Dust will fall back
into the eyes of those
who throw dust toward the sun.

## March 5.

Man creates his own disharmony.

## March 6.

The real abode of God is in the heart of man.
When it is frozen with bitterness or hatred
the doors of the shrine are closed
and the light is hidden.

**March 7.**

It is a false love
that does not uproot man's claim of 'I.'
The first and last lesson of love is 'I am not.'

**March 8.**

You cannot be both horse and rider at the same
time.

**March 9.**

It is more important to know the truth about
one's self than to try to find out the truth
of heaven and hell.

**March 10.**

Every man's pursuit is according to his evolution.

**March 11.**

Man sees what he sees; he cannot see beyond it.

**March 12.**

The source of truth is within man.
He himself is the object of his realisation.

**March 13.**

As life unfolds itself to man
the first lesson he learns is humility.

**March 14.**

God is truth and truth is God.

**March 15.**

Until man loses himself in the vision of God
he cannot be said to really live.

**March 16.**

At every step of evolution
man's realisation of God changes.

**March 17.**

Verily he is victorious who has conquered himself.

**March 18.**

Prayer is the greatest virtue, and
the only way of being free from all sin.

**March 19.**

It is the sincere devotee who knows best
how to humble himself before God.


**March 20.**

It is wise to see all things
and yet to turn our eyes
from all that should be overlooked.


**March 21.**

Our soul is blessed with the impression of the
glory of God whenever our lips praise him.

**March 22.**

There is one teacher – God himself.
We are all his pupils.

**March 23.**

All earthly knowledge is as a cloud
covering the sun.

**March 24.**

The first sign of the
realisation of truth
is tolerance.

**March 25.**

He who is filled
with the knowledge of names and forms
has no capacity for the knowledge of God.

**March 26.**

Man is closer to God
than the fishes are to the ocean.

**March 27.**

Patience is a process
through which a soul goes,
in order to become precious.

**March 28.**

Until the heart is empty
it cannot receive the knowledge of God.

**March 29.**

According to his evolution,
man knows truth.

**March 30.**

We can never sufficiently humble our limited
selves before limitless perfection.

## March 31.

Even to utter the name of God
is a blessing that can fill the soul
with light and joy and happiness
as nothing else can do.

## April 1.

When one praises the beauty of God,
the soul is filled with bliss.

## April 2.

Sympathy is the root of religion,
and as long as the spirit of sympathy
is living in your heart
you have the light of religion.

**April 3.**

Life is a misery for the man absorbed in himself.

**April 4.**

To give sympathy is sovereignty,
to desire it from others is captivity.

**April 5.**

God speaks to the ears of every heart,
but it is not every heart that hears him.

## April 6.

As one can see when the eyes are open,
so one can understand when the heart is open.

## April 7.

It is being dead to self
that is the recognition of God.

## April 8.

As the light of the sun helps the plant to grow,
so the divine spirit
helps the soul toward its perfection.

**April 9.**

Things are worthwhile when we seek them,
for only then do we know their value.

**April 10.**

When a man looks at the ocean
he can only see that part of it
which comes within his range of vision.
So it is with the truth.

**April 11.**

It does not matter in what way a person offers his
respect and his reverence to the deity he worships:
it matters only how sincere he is in his offering.

**April 12.**

The ideal of God is a bridge connecting the
limited life with the unlimited; whoever
travels over this bridge passes safely from
the limited to the unlimited life.

**April 13.**

He who wants to understand will understand.

**April 14.**

Man is the picture
of the reflection of his imagination.
He is as large or as small as he thinks himself.

**April 15.**

The great teachers of humanity
become streams of love.

**April 16.**

'God is love': three words which open up
an unending realm for the thinker
who desires to probe
the depths of the secret of life.

**April 17.**

It is the surface of the sea
which makes waves and roaring breakers;
the depth is silent.

**April 18.**

Our success or failure depends
upon the harmony or disharmony
of our individual will with the divine will.

**April 19.**

The wave realises 'I am the sea',
and by falling into the sea
prostrates itself to its god.

**April 20.**

The secret of happiness is hidden under
the cover of spiritual knowledge.

**April 21.**

When the soul is first born into the false self, it is blind. In the true self the soul opens its eyes.

**April 22.**

To learn the lesson of how to live
is more important
than any psychic or occult learning.

**April 23.**

Knowledge without love is lifeless.

**April 24.**

The aim of the mystic
is to keep near the idea of unity
and find out where we unite.




**April 25.**

Sleep is comfortable
but awakening is interesting.




**April 26.**

Every moment has its special message.

**April 27.**

To make God a reality
is the real object of worship.

**April 28.**

Every passion, every emotion,
has its effect upon the mind.
Every change of mind, however slight,
has its effect upon man's body.

**April 29.**

When souls meet each other, what truth they can
exchange! It is uttered in silence, yet always
surely reaches its goal.

**April 30.**

All gains, whether material, spiritual, moral
or mystical are in answer to one's own character.

**May 1.**

You can have all good things - wealth, friends,
kindness, love to give and love to receive - once
you have learned not to be blinded by them,
learned to escape from disappointment and
repugnance at the idea that things are not
as you want them to be.

**May 2.**

The truth need not be veiled,
for it veils itself from the eyes of the ignorant.

**May 3.**

No man should allow his mind to be
a vehicle for others to use. He who
does not direct his own mind lacks mastery.


**May 4.**

Rest of mind is as necessary as rest of body
and yet we always keep the former in action.


**May 5.**

Those who have given deep thoughts to the world
are those who have controlled
the activity of their minds.

**May 6.**

Unity in realisation
is far greater than unity in variety.


**May 7.**

The after-life is like a gramophone. Man's mind
brings the records; if they are hard
the instrument produces harsh notes,
if beautiful, then it will sing beautiful songs.
It will produce the same records
that man has experienced in this life.


**May 8.**

He who depends upon his eyes for sight,
his ears for hearing and his mouth for speech,–
he is still dead.

**May 9.**

We cover our spirit under our body, our light
under a bushel. We never allow the spirit
to become conscious of itself.

**May 10.**

When we devote ourselves to the thought of God
all illumination and revelation is ours.

**May 11.**

God communication
is the best communication
that true spiritualism can teach us.

**May 12.**

The mystic desires what Omar Khayyam calls
wine, the wine of the Christ. After drinking
this wine, one will never thirst.


**May 13.**

Our limited self is a wall
separating us from the self of God.


**May 14.**

The wisdom and justice of God are within us
and yet they are far away,
hidden by the veil of the limited self.

**May 15.**

He who is looking for a reward
is smaller than his reward;
he who has renounced a thing has risen above it.


**May 16.**

The poverty of one who has renounced
is real riches, compared with the riches
of one who holds them fast.


**May 17.**

Love for God is the expansion of the heart,
and all actions that come from the lover of God
are virtues; they cannot be otherwise.

**May 18.**

God is the ideal that raises mankind
to the utmost height of perfection.

**May 19.**

He is wise who treats an acquaintance as a friend,
he is foolish who treats a friend
as an acquaintance, and he is impossible
who treats friends and acquaintances
as strangers: you cannot help him.

**May 20.**

Insight into life is the real religion
which alone can help men to understand life.

**May 21.**

The realisation that the whole of life must be
give and take is the realisation of
the spiritual truth and fact of true democracy.
Not until this spirit is formed in the individual
can the whole world be elevated to the higher
grade.


**May 22.**

The perfect life is following one's own ideal,
not in checking those of others.
Leave everyone to follow his own ideal.


**May 23.**

Every man's desire is according to his evolution.
That for which he is ready
is the desirable thing for him.

54

**May 24.**

Discussion is for those who say,
'What I say is right, and what you say is wrong.'
A sage never says such a thing,
hence there is no discussion.


**May 25.**

Tolerance does not come by learning but by
insight, by understanding that each one should
be allowed to travel along the path which is
suited to his temperament.


**May 26.**

As long as a man has a longing
to obtain any particular object
he cannot go further than that object.

**May 27.**

Every man's path is for himself.
Let him accomplish his own desires
that he may be able to rise above them
to the eternal goal.

**May 28.**

The control of self
means the control of everything.

**May 29.**

God is love.
When love is awakened in the heart
God is awakened there.

**May 30.**

All the disharmony of the world caused by
religious differences is the result of man's
failure to understand that religion is one,
truth is one, God is one: how can there be
two religions?

**May 31.**

The use of friendship for selfish motive
is like mixing bitter poison
with sweet rose syrup.

**June 1.**

Man's bodily appetites take him away
from his heart's desire.
His heart's desires keep him away
from the abode of his soul.

**June 2.**

Words are but the shadows
of thoughts and feelings.

**June 3.**

The more elevated the soul,
the broader is the outlook.

**June 4.**

The secret of a friend
should be kept as one's own secret.
The fault of a friend
one should hide as one's own fault.

**June 5.**

Forbearance, patience and tolerance
are the only conditions
which keep two individual hearts united.

**June 6.**

We blame others for our sorrows and misfortunes,
not perceiving that we ourselves
are the creators of our world.

**June 7.**

Nobody appears inferior to us
when our heart is kindled with kindness
and our eyes are open to the vision of God.

**June 8.**

Selfishness keeps man blind through life.

**June 9.**

For every soul the final victory
in the battle of life comes
when he has risen above the things
which he once most valued.

**June 10.**

When power leads and wisdom follows
the face of wisdom is veiled and she stumbles.
When wisdom leads and power follows,
they arrive safely at their destination.

**June 11.**

Man's whole conduct in life
depends upon what he holds in his thought.


**June 12.**

He who can be detached enough to keep his eyes
open to all those whom circumstances have
placed about him and see in what way he can be
of help to them, he it is who becomes rich,
he inherits the kingdom of God.


**June 13.**

True justice cannot be perceived until the veil
of selfishness has been removed from the eyes.

**June 14.**

Our thoughts have prepared for us
the happiness or unhappiness we experience.

**June 15.**

Love is the best means of making the heart
capable of reflecting the power of the soul;
love in the sense of pain rather than pleasure.
Every blow opens a door
from where the soul power comes forth.

**June 16.**

Every experience on the physical,
astral or mental plane is just a dream
before the soul.

**June 17.**

The fire of devotion
purifies the heart of the devotee,
and brings spiritual freedom.

**June 18.**

When love's fire produces its flame, it illuminates
like a torch the devotee's path in life,
and all darkness vanishes.

**June 19.**

It is mistrust that misleads.
Sincerity always leads straight to the goal.

**June 20.**

Love lies in service. Only that which is done
not for fame or name, nor for the appreciation
or thanks of those for whom it is done,
is love's service.

**June 21.**

The soul is all light. Darkness
is caused by the deadness of the heart;
pain makes it alive.

**June 22.**

The quality of forgiveness
that burns up all things except beauty,
is the quality of love.

**June 23.**

Each individual composes the music of his own life. If he injures another he breaks the harmony, and there is discord in the melody of his life.

**June 24.**

He who with sincerity
seeks his real purpose in life
is himself sought by that purpose.

**June 25.**

Through motion and change
life becomes intelligible.
We live a life of change
but it is constancy we seek.
It is this innate desire of the soul
that leads man to God.

**June 26.**

Every being has a definite vocation, and his vocation is the light that illumines his life. The man who disregards his vocation is a lamp unlit.

**June 27.**

The heart sleeps
until it is awakened to life by a blow.
It is as a rock, and the hidden fire
flashes out when struck by another rock.

**June 28.**

The awakened heart says, 'I must give,
I must not demand.' Thus it enters a gate
that leads to a constant happiness.

**June 29.**

The worlds are held together by the heat of the
sun. Each of us is an atom, held in position by the
eternal sun we call God. Within us is the same
central power we call the light or the love of God.
With it we hold together the human beings within
our sphere, or, lacking it, we let them fall.


**June 30.**

When a man dives within,
he finds that his real self
is above the perpetual motion of the universe.


**July 1.**

Man's pride and satisfaction in what he knows
limits the scope of his vision.

**July 2.**

Man must first create peace in himself
if he desires to see peace in the world,
for, lacking peace within,
no effort of his can bring any result.

**July 3.**

The knowledge of self is the essential knowledge;
it gives knowledge of humanity.
In the understanding of the human being
lies that understanding of nature
which reveals the law of creation.

**July 4.**

While man blames another for causing him harm,
the wise man first takes himself to task.

## July 5.

The wise, whatever their faith,
have always been able to meet each other
beyond those boundaries of external forms
and conventions which are natural
and necessary to human life,
but which nonetheless separate humanity.


## July 6.

The message proves the messenger, not the claim.


## July 7.

Every soul has a definite task,
and the fulfillment of each individual purpose
can alone lead man aright.
Illumination comes to him through the medium
of his own talent.

**July 8.**

While man judges another
from his own moral standpoint,
the wise man looks also
at the point of view of another.


**July 9.**

While man rejoices over his rise
and sorrows over his fall,
the wise man takes both
as the natural consequences of life.


**July 10.**

It is the lover of God,
whose heart is filled with devotion,
who can commune with God.
Not he who makes an effort
with his intellect to analyse God.

**July 11.**

Do not bemoan the past,
do not worry about the future,-
try to make the best of today.

**July 12.**

He who can quicken the feeling of another
to joy or to gratitude, by that much
he adds to his own life.

**July 13.**

Praise cannot exist without blame.
It has no existence without its opposite.

**July 14.**

Riches and power may vanish
because they are outside ourselves.
Only that which is within can we call our own.


**July 15.**

The world is evolving from imperfection towards
perfection; it needs all love and sympathy. Great
tenderness and watchfulness is required from each
one of us.


**July 16.**

The heart of every man, both good and bad,
is the abode of God, and care should be taken
never to wound anyone by word or act.

**July 17.**

We should be careful to take away from ourselves
any thorns that prick us
in the personality of others.


**July 18.**

There is a light within every soul. It only needs
the clouds that overshadow it to be broken
for it to beam forth.


**July 19.**

The soul's true happiness lies in experiencing the
inner joy, and it will never be fully satisfied
with outer, seeming pleasures. Its connection is
with God, and nothing short of perfection will
ever satisfy it.

**July 20.**

Every blow in life pierces the heart and awakens
our feelings to sympathise with others.
Every swing of comfort lulls us to sleep,
and we become unaware of all.

**July 21.**

A study of life is the greatest of all religions;
there is no greater or more interesting study.

**July 22.**

We can learn virtue from the greatest sinner
if we consider him as a teacher.

**July 23.**

Warmth melts, while cold freezes. A drop of ice
in a warm place spreads and covers a larger space,
whereas a drop of water in a cold place freezes
and becomes limited.
Repentance has the effect
of spreading a drop in a warm sphere,
causing the heart to expand and become universal,
while the hardening of the heart brings limitation.

**July 24.**

There should be a balance in all our actions;
to be either extreme or lukewarm is equally bad.

**July 25.**

Our spirit is the real part of us, our body its garment. A man would not find peace at the tailor's because his coat comes from there: neither can the spirit obtain true happiness from the earth just because his body belongs to earth.

**July 26.**

Every purpose has a birth and death, therefore God is beyond purpose.

**July 27.**

Belief and disbelief have divided man
into so many sects, blinding his eyes
to the vision of the oneness of all life.

**July 28.**

Spirit can only love spirit; in loving form
it deludes itself.

**July 29.**

To love is one thing, to understand is another.
He who loves is a devotee,
but he who understands is a friend.

**July 30.**

Among a million believers in God
there is scarcely one
who makes God a reality.


**July 31.**

The soul feels suffocated
when the doors of the heart are closed.


**August 1.**

Understanding
makes the trouble of life lighter to bear.

**August 2.**

The same herb planted in various atmospheric conditions will vary in form accordingly but will retain its characteristics.

**August 3.**

Think, before envying the position of your fellow man, with what difficulty he has arrived at it.

**August 4.**

Life is what it is;
you cannot change it
but you can always change yourself.

**August 5.**

Life is a continual series of experiences,
one leading to the other
until the soul arrives at its destination.

**August 6.**

External life is the shadow of the inner reality.

**August 7.**

At the cost of one failure, the wise can
learn a lesson for a whole lifetime.

**August 8.**

The more you evolve spiritually, the further
you pass from the understanding of every man.

**August 9.**

One word can be more precious
than all the treasures of earth.

**August 10.**

Narrowness is primitiveness.
It is the breadth of heart that proves evolution.

**August 11.**

It is simpler to find a way to heaven
than to find a way on earth.

**August 12.**

It is God who, with the hands of man, designs
and carries out his intended plans in nature.

**August 13.**

The lover of nature is the true worshipper of God.

**August 14.**

In the country you see the glory of God,
in the city you glorify his name.

**August 15.**

The pain of life is the price paid
for the quickening of the heart.

**August 16.**

Words that enlighten the soul
are more precious than jewels.

**August 17.**

Love is the current coin
of all peoples in all periods.

**August 18.**

Do not take the example of another
as an excuse for your own wrong-doing.

**August 19.**

Overlook the greatest fault of another, but do not
partake of it yourself in the smallest degree.

## August 20.

Cleverness and complexity
are not necessarily wisdom.

## August 21.

The whole world's treasure is too small a price
to pay for a word that kindles the soul.

## August 22.

He is living whose sympathy is awake,
he is dead whose heart is asleep.

**August 23.**

By our thoughts we have prepared for ourselves
the happiness or unhappiness we experience.

**August 24.**

Put your trust in God for support
and see his hidden hand
working through all sources.

**August 25.**

Faith is the abc of the realisation of God.
This faith begins by prayer.

## August 26.

Passion is the smoke and emotion the glow
of love's fire; unselfishness is the flame
that illumines the path.

## August 27.

The soul of Christ is the light of the universe.

## August 28.

Death is a tax the soul has to pay
for having had a name and a form.

**August 29.**

A pure life and a clean conscience
are as two wings attached to the soul.

**August 30.**

The giver is greater than the gift.

**August 31.**

He who has spent has used,
he who has collected has lost,
but he who has given
has saved his treasure forever.

### September 1.

Joy and sorrow both are for each other.
If it were not for joy, sorrow could not be,
and if it were not for sorrow,
joy could not be experienced.

### September 2.

Self-pity is the cause of all life's grievances.

### September 3.

How can the unlimited being be limited?
All that seems limited is in its depth
beyond all limitations.

**September 4.**

Pleasure blocks, but pain
clears the way of inspiration.

**September 5.**

There is no source of happiness
other than that in the heart of man.

**September 6.**

Happy is he who does good to others;
miserable is he who expects good from others.

**September 7.**

One virtue is more powerful than a thousand vices.

**September 8.**

The soul is either raised or cast down
by the power of its own thought, speech and
action.

**September 9.**

Love is the divine mother's arms; when those arms
are spread, every soul falls into them.

**September 10.**

It is the fruit that makes the tree bow low.

**September 11.**

In order to learn forgiveness,
man must first learn tolerance.

**September 12.**

The first step towards forgiveness is to forget.

## September 13.

The only way to live in the midst of inharmonious
influences is to strengthen the will-power and
endure all things, yet keep fineness of character
and nobility of manner together with an ever
living heart full of love.

## September 14.

Devotion to a spiritual teacher
is not for the sake of the teacher,
it is for God.

## September 15.

To become cold from the coldness
of the world is weakness,
to become broken by the hardness
of the world is feebleness,
but to live in the world and yet to keep above it
is like walking on the water.

**September 16.**

God alone deserves all love
and the freedom of love is in giving it to God.

**September 17.**

Love has the power
to open the door of eternal life.

**September 18.**

Love has its limitations
when it is directed towards limited beings;
love directed to God has no limitations.

## September 19.

The teacher, however great, can never
give his knowledge to the pupil;
the pupil must create his own knowledge.

## September 20.

One thing is true: although the teacher
cannot give the knowledge, he can kindle the light
if the oil is in the lamp.

## September 21.

Will power is the keynote of mastery;
asceticism is the development of will-power.

## September 22.

Real generosity is an unfailing sign of spirituality.

**September 23.**

There are two kinds of generosity, the real
and the shadow. The former is prompted by love,
the latter by vanity.

**September 24.**

It is better to pay than receive from the vain,
for such favours demand ten times their cost.

**September 25.**

The kingdom of heaven is in the hearts
of those who realise God.

**September 26.**

In order to relieve the hunger of others
we must forget our own hunger.


**September 27.**

It is when man has lost the idea of separateness
and feels himself at one with all creation
that his eyes are opened
and he sees the cause of all things.


**September 28.**

To fall beneath one's ideal
is to lose one's share of life.

**September 29.**

The wise of all ages have taught
that it is knowledge of the divine being
that is life, and the only reality.


**September 30.**

When the stream of love flows in its full strength,
it purifies all that stands in its way,
as the Ganges – according to the teaching
of the ancients – purifies all those
who plunge into its sacred waters.


**October 1.**

Each soul's attainment is according
to its evolution.

**October 2.**

You must sacrifice
something very dear to you
when His call comes.

**October 3.**

Renunciation is always for a purpose:
it is to kindle the soul
that nothing may hold it back from God.
But once it is kindled,
the life of renunciation is not necessary.

**October 4.**

There are those who, like a lighted candle,
can light other candles. But the other candles
must be of wax; if they are of steel
they cannot be lighted.

**October 5.**

There is no greater scripture than nature,
for nature is life itself.


**October 6.**

Wisdom can be learnt only gradually,
and not every soul is ready
to receive or to understand
the complexity of the purpose of life.


**October 7.**

It is a very high stage on the path of love
when one really learns to love another
with a love that asks no return.

**October 8.**

Love alone is the fountain
from which all virtues fall
as drops of sparkling water.

**October 9.**

The whole purpose of life is
to make God a reality.

**October 10.**

If you seek the good in every soul,
you will always find it. For God is in all things;
still more, he is in all beings.

**October 11.**

The knowledge of God is beyond man's reason.
The secret of God is hidden
in the knowledge of unity.

**October 12.**

Seek him in all souls, good or bad, wise
and foolish, attractive and unattractive;
in the depths of each there is God.

**October 13.**

When in ourselves there is inharmony,
how can we spread harmony?

**October 14.**

The innermost being of man
is the real being of God.

**October 15.**

Love itself is the healing power
and the remedy for all pain.

**October 16.**

By loving, forgiving and serving, it is possible
for your whole life to become one single vision
of the sublime beauty of God.

**October 17.**

Mysticism
to the mystic
is both science and religion.



**October 18.**

The principles of mysticism
rise from the heart of man;
they are learnt by intuition and proved by reason.



**October 19.**

Your work in life must be your religion,
whatever your occupation may be.

**October 20.**

The true joy of every soul is in the realisation
of the divine spirit; the absence of realisation
keeps the soul in despair.

**October 21.**

Beyond the narrow barriers of race and creed
we can all unite,
because we all belong to one God.

**October 22.**

All forms of worship or prayer
must draw man closer to God.

## October 23.

When man is separated from God in his thought,
his belief is of no use,
his worship of little use.

## October 24.

The source of the realisation of truth
is within man; he himself is the object
of his realisation.

## October 25.

True self-denial is losing one's self in God.

**October 26.**

Many do good, but how few do it wisely!
To do good wisely is the work of the sage.

**October 27.**

According to his evolution, man knows the truth,
and the more he knows,
the more he finds there is to know.

**October 28.**

There is nothing in the world
which is not the instrument of God.

**October 29.**

Man mistakes when he begins
to cultivate the heart
by wanting to sow the seed himself
instead of leaving the sowing to God.

**October 30.**

Friends, we start our lives as teachers, and it is
very hard for us to learn to become pupils. There
are many whose only difficulty in life is that
they are teachers already. What we have to learn is
pupilship. There is but one teacher, God himself.

**October 31.**

Earthly knowledge is as clouds dimming the sight,
and it is the breaking of these clouds
– in other words, purity of heart – that gives
the capacity for the knowledge of God to rise.

108

**November 1.**

Self stands as a wall
between man and God.


**November 2.**

It is a patient pursuit to bring water
from the depth of the ground;
one has to deal with much mud in digging
before one reaches the water of life.


**November 3.**

In man's search for truth, the first lesson
and the last is love. There must be no separation.
No 'I am, and thou art not.' Until man has arrived
at that selfless consciousness
he cannot know life and truth.

**November 4.**

By the power of prayer man opens the door of the heart, in which God, the ever-forgiving, the all-merciful, abides.

**November 5.**

To be really sorry for one's errors
is like opening the doors of heaven.

**November 6.**

One must not make even principles so set that one cannot alter them.

## November 7.

As a child learning to walk falls
a thousand times before he can stand,
and after that falls again and again
until at last he can walk, so are we
as little children before God.

## November 8.

Self-denial is not renouncing things,
it is denying the self,
and the first lesson of self-denial is humility.

## November 9.

The more elevated the soul,
the broader the outlook.

## November 10.

Mastery lies not merely in stilling the mind, but in directing it towards whatever point you desire.

## November 11.

God is love; so God is beyond the law,
for love is above the law.

## November 12.

When the body and the mind are restless,
nothing in life can be accomplished.
Success is the result of control.

**November 13.**

When speech is controlled, the eyes speak;
the glance says what words can never say.

**November 14.**

The better the instrument
the greater the satisfaction of the soul.

**November 15.**

Wisdom is not in words, it is in understanding.

**November 16.**

The message of God is like a spring of water:
it rises and falls, and makes its way by itself.


**November 17.**

If the eyes and ears are open, the leaves
of the trees become as pages of the Bible.


**November 18.**

The soul of all is one soul, and the truth
is one truth, under whatever religion it is hidden.


114

## November 19.

Narrowness is not necessarily devotion,
but often appears so.

## November 20.

It is the soul's light
which is natural intelligence.

## November 21.

The wave is the sea itself,
yet when it rises in the form of a wave
it is the wave,
and when you look at the whole of it, it is the sea.

**November 22.**

It is not the solid wood that can become a flute,
it is the empty reed.

**November 23.**

Reason is learned from the ever-changing world
but true knowledge comes from the essence of life.

**November 24.**

God is within you. You are his instrument
and through you he expresses himself
to the external world.

**November 25.**

It is according to the extent
of our consciousness of prayer
that our prayer reaches God.

**November 26.**

The heart must be empty in order
to receive the knowledge of God.

**November 27.**

As long as in love there is 'you' and 'me',
love is not fully kindled.

**November 28.**

Once you have given up your limited self willingly
to the unlimited, you will rejoice so much
in that consciousness that you will not care
to be small again.

**November 29.**

The deeper your prayers echo
in your own consciousness
the more audible they are to God.

**November 30.**

It is depth of thought that is powerful,
and sincerity of feeling which creates atmosphere.

## December 1.

The higher you rise,
the wider the margin of your view.


## December 2.

Justice can never be developed
while we judge others.
The only way is by constantly judging ourselves.


## December 3.

Joy and sorrow are the light
and shade of life.
Without light and shade no picture is clear.

### December 4.

The wise man submits to conditions
when he is helpless, bowing to the will of God.
But the evil that is avoidable he roots out
without sparing one single moment or effort.

### December 5.

Enviable is he who loves and asks no return.

### December 6.

To deny the changeableness of life
is like fancying a motionless sea,
which can only exist in one's imagination.

**December 7.**

Learn to live a true life
and you will know the truth.

**December 8.**

Wisdom is attained in solitude.

**December 9.**

The seeming death of the body
is the real birth of the soul.

**December 10.**

As the rose blooms amidst thorns,
so great souls shine out through all opposition.



**December 11.**

When the artist loses himself in his art,
then the art comes to life.



**December 12.**

Do nothing with fear
and fear not whatever you do.


122

**December 13.**

Love develops into harmony,
and of harmony is beauty born.

**December 14.**

He who keeps no secrets has no depth in his
heart.

**December 15.**

Behind us all is one spirit and one life.
How then can we be happy if our neighbour
is not also happy?

**December 16.**

The sea of life is in constant motion; no one can
stop its ever-moving waves. The master walks over
the waves, the wise man swims in the water, but
the ignorant man is drowned in his effort to cross.

**December 17.**

Man's greatest privilege
is to become a suitable instrument of God.

**December 18.**

The trees of the forest
silently await God's blessing.

### December 19.

The plain truth is too simple
for the seeker after complexity,
who is looking for things he cannot understand.

### December 20.

An unsuccessful man often keeps success away
by the impression of his former failures.

### December 21.

Man himself is the tree of desire,
and the root of that tree is in his own heart.

**December 22.**

With goodwill and trust in God, self-confidence
and a hopeful attitude towards life,
a man can always win his battle, however difficult.


**December 23.**

There are many paths, and each man
considers his own the best and wisest.
Let each one choose that
which belongs to his own temperament.


**December 24.**

Failure, either in health or affairs,
means there has been lack of self-control.


126

**December 25.**

No soul perishes.
The soul was not born to perish.

**December 26.**

Love is unlimited, but it needs scope to expand
and rise; without that scope life is unhappy.

**December 27.**

Every wave of the sea, as it rises, seems
to be stretching its hands upwards, as if
to say take me up higher and higher.

**December 28.**

True pleasure
lies in the sharing of joy with another.

**December 29.**

A gain or loss which is momentary is not real. If
we knew reality we should never grieve over the
loss of anything which experience shows to be
only transitory.

**December 30.**

A soul is as great as the circle of its influence.

**December 31.**

Happiness lies in thinking or doing
that which one considers beautiful.

Printed in the USA
CPSIA information can be obtained
at www.ICGtesting.com
JSHW082219140824
68134JS00015B/629

9 780900 217128